Somewhere Far
Joe Carrick-Varty

smith|doorstop

Published 2019 by Smith|Doorstop Books
The Poetry Business
Campo House,
54 Campo Lane,
Sheffield S1 2EG
www.poetrybusiness.co.uk

Copyright © Joe Carrick-Varty 2019
All Rights Reserved

ISBN 978-1-912196-69-2
Designed & Typeset by Utter
Author photo: Alexander Fahey
Printed by Biddles

Smith|Doorstop books are a member of Inpress: www.inpressbooks.co.uk. Distributed by NBN International, Airport Business Centre, 10 Thornbury Road Plymouth PL 6 7PP.

The Poetry Business gratefully acknowledges the support of Arts Council England.

Contents

5	Parks
6	Somewhere Far
7	In Amber
8	Your Bicycle
9	Drowning in Wembley Stadium
10	Reef
11	Skip
12	A week and not a word since the argument
13	Eagle River, 2017
14	Swing Set
16	At the end
17	Third Date
18	The Discovery
19	All of a Sudden
20	My father is sitting on the other side of the french doors
22	Shopping for Sunglasses in November
23	Leaves
24	The First and Last Day of Everything
25	Ross 154
26	Lop Nur
27	Moonless June
28	When you lean close and tell me
29	Feathers
30	The Secret
31	Impacts
33	Acknowledgements

I was yea high and muddy
Lookin' for what was lookin' for me
– Mac Miller

Parks
For Caitlin

For the hour it takes to write this poem
I'll believe the pigeon in Brookes library
is my father's mind, back for a weekend,
delivered to my sister and me
in the shape of his face, his beanie hat,
the quick glint of his silver earring.

My father's mind hides in plain sight,
waving from a picnic bench in a busy park,
his perfectly timed smile a trick of skin –
another afternoon of swings and slides.
I believe the pigeon is my father's mind
because no one else has spotted it

perched up there on the light fitting, cooing.
If I have it right, if I know our father,
the pigeon will be gone by morning,
ushered out by some cleaner. And then
for the rest of the week the bird is nowhere
and everywhere we look.

Somewhere Far

Walking back from nursery
down Cornmarket to the shop on Ship Street,
You wait out here now and then a pen,
one of those little blue ones,
draw me something nice,
betting slips, twenty of them.

And when I'd finished the first batch
out you came with more,
Very nice and *I like that one,*
maybe a Refresher or two.
Men passing on the step
smiled or nodded or shuffled

but mostly they said nothing
because I was as much a part of that place
as any of the footballers on the walls,
or the fruit machines, or the
commentators, or the screens
where you would stand

when you thought I couldn't see,
Don't come in, you mustn't come in,
tapping your foot, hands in pockets,
face turned up at the horses
making their way from left to right
across the green light of somewhere

far from here.

In Amber

In my dream you are almost drunk,
struggling with the lock on the french doors
of my childhood, a lit cigarette
cupped in your palm.

Seconds before I wake, I realise
I've no idea which side you're on, which side
of those huge lime-scaled sheets of glass
you huddle to, hunched and cursing

the key which catches as you turn it. Sure,
the garden lurks behind, the gravel path,
but so does the television, the empty fish tank,
the cat's water bowl. So, which side are you on,

and where does that leave me?
Give me a clue – nod, blink, catch my eye,
crunch a snail shell, ash your cigarette,
flick the butt so I might hear it land.

If I could reach I'd pluck a silver hair from your arm,
just one, like a dream's very own pinch,
a dream we'll both wake from, at the same time,
on the sofa, some film playing ... *Did you feel it too?*

Your Bicycle

That morning in 1993, the lawn misting,
unkept at the wall where we'd dug the hole
for the pond that we abandoned,
your bicycle, with spokes and chain

grown through, tangled, leant by itself.
The shape it left lasted a second;
first the wheels, then the pedals
stiff and locked, rusted, stuck to the honeysuckle

curled on the frame. Might the garden be in on this?
Might you, one day, come home, step out
over the gravel, ducking the rosebush
to find nothing but the jungle I haven't weeded since?

Or might you know already
about the snail I found there, about the webs
hung between the rubber handle and the wall,
the bell full up with lichen, moss, earwigs,

those woodlice in the brake pads?
The grass tugged a little, and let go with a slow rip.
Uprooted, then coiling back into place
like a fist so intent on keeping hold.

Drowning in Wembley Stadium

If you chained yourself to the top-most seat
on the top-most tier of Wembley Stadium
and one drop of rain fell on the centre circle,
then two drops, then four drops,
doubling every minute,
how long would it be before you drowned?
Twelve hours.
So, that last minute,
the last of the seven hundred twenty,
eleven hours fifty-nine,
the second before that last minute,
how full would the stadium be?
It would be half full.
At eleven hours fifty nine
the water would be fifty metres from your throat,
it might resemble a swimming pool, or a lake
with ripples, yes, plastic bags,
a reflection of the sun, a flock passing,
then the wind might hush,
that sun disappear,
traffic on Rutherford Way or Falton Road might stop,
look up at the ocean emptying out of the sky,
think to themselves,
'I hope nobody's in there.'

Reef

They call this place a reef. Walk a few hundred paces
and you reach roads, buses, direction. There are

fields too, horses, a wooden fence opposite a church,
a wall where children line up each Sunday. Now, why a reef?

Maybe you'll recognise it. Maybe you'll spot the moment
light filters through a break in cloud and fills

a dual carriageway, a school hall, an underpass.
Maybe you'll hear a plane bank over train tracks,

bridges, a supermarket car park
catching its shadow on the concrete

and remember the time water existed here,
the time the horizon was the end,

the time stingrays passed in silence.
And – if you get this far – we'll guess it was you.

The first to unstick an eyelid, blink in the darkness.
Yes, you who told us to 'Come, come this way'

offering a hand and pointing towards the light, asking us to walk
when the sand at our feet was nothing but shells

broken and broken a thousand times.

Skip

It was as if a giant turtle – the last of its kind –
had realised this pale street was not for him,

the grey buildings, the black lichen,
the dull-hum, orange-swamp at night

towed his dreams: lapis lazuli, indigo currents
for moonbeams, soft, mercury,

and in a moment,
forgot all about his shell, its weighted roof,

and flopped in drunken footsteps
towards the sea.

A week and not a word since the argument

I'm cycling near your house,
cycling for no reason, to nowhere,
but I'm near your house, on your road in fact,
passing the Baptist Church
and the redbrick half-finished new build
and in no time at all the shape of you is walking towards me
slap bang in the middle of the road.
We talk, albeit gingerly, about my work at the playscheme,
about the kids who fight there,
about my sister off to Uni in a month –
to Glasgow! As if she could've picked a further place.
You slur only a little when you say that.
Where you off anyway?
Nowhere.

The barman you call Mason nods,
unlocks the side door, props it open,
motions you inside. I look at my watch: 11 a.m. –
I'm seven years old, waiting with a Coke outside
the frosted glass of The Seven Stars,
smelling cigarettes every time the door bangs –
then I'm you, in Coventry, your father
at the bar, more hair than the both of us, taller
in the backlit glow of the doorway
than I'd known him from the black and white photo
you stuck to the fridge one Christmas Eve.
You gather us around, whiskey-whisper *this is your Grandad*,
no liver cirrhosis, not dead at 48,
still bringing pork scratchings and a bottle of fizzy pop
to land with a clink on the step.

So, you coming in or not?

Eagle River, 2017

Home one morning to find my hat and gloves
hard with frost on the spade handle.
Maybe you'd take my silence for a green
the sun gives to the shadowgrass.
And, as you boil the kettle to melt the drain
I'd watch a whole life come and go
in the very place I waited:
pruning shears, a wheelbarrow,
a rake, a hose wound halfway –

there you go –
bending to where a stepladder,
unfolded all summer, made perfect
stepping stones in the hard-packed light.

Swing Set

We share a cigarette in your parents'
empty living room, taking turns to ash in a mug

you decided to keep at the last minute.
The beige folding chairs are the last to go,

('hunkajunk'), as you recount your mother
unfolding them every night before the news.

But, with the three blokes gone, their tea bags in the sink
and the van bleep bleeping its way down the drive

you say 'fuck it' and we're back in the chairs,
lighting another cigarette, ashing in the same mug.

Later, we'll unfold them somewhere else
and watch a house first make its hard line on the lawn

and I'll have you tell me over and over
about underground oceans on Jupiter,

about gas clouds three-light-years-tall,
about atoms of light as if light were grass

I could bend towards, run my fingers through.
There is a moment when the shadow of a house

leaves just a piece of lawn. But we weren't to know.
In a few short minutes the shape of this house

will disappear up the back wall
where a yellow swing set peeps over

and the top half of a child appears again,
and again, and again, older each time

and on a whole different kind of orbit
which is really all I've been meaning to say.

At the end

of that grass path, you know,
the one you cross the Ring Road to reach,
past the sign for the golf course, its *panoramic views of Oxford*

and the turning for Chilswell
as if you're headed for the garden centre; more specifically
for those two black pools by the entrance
and the rainbow trout they keep;

that penny sweet machine full of fish feed
all *pit stop*, all *poke our heads in*, all *we'll only be a minute*
before the real climb began,
before tarmac gave way to pebbles then grass, freshly mown –

and by whom? At the end of all this
is the bench I'm sitting on now. So I thought I'd tell you,
your plaque is rusting a little, in one corner.
And I've just today picked my spot.

Third Date

We could be any of these couples –
two, three, five years in, married, dog, kids, the lot.
We could be here discussing a mortgage,
an attic extension, or, ahead of *our turn to host*, deciding on pad thai –
Karen posted a number for a great babysitter.
Our friends (all professionals, all city people)
might walk this park too.
We might bump into them.
Our kids could all take the 2A to school,
play football on wet Saturday mornings for the team
with the red and black kit, the bravest of us
on the touchline, shouting along, blowing into polystyrene cups.

Up close, out here, you and I without a drink, without
the buffer of a screen, without time
to type a good reply, just the crunch
of our footsteps on this gravel path,
the line of oak trees with the cricket pitch behind,
your mouth cuts a far cry from the place I got to know so well
last Wednesday, under a Hackney bus stop.
Until I brush your arm, as if by accident,
and the silence that's opened up between us no longer screams *life*,
and a collie dog off the lead whizzes past,
and the distant tennis players call it a day
but I doubt you've noticed.

The Discovery
For Bill Guastalla

The town has stopped.
I am cycling no-handed down Levenshulme hill,
through the cones and cement mixers circled
in the junction and its roundabout
dovetailed from view of the bridge
and the wind on my palms was the *three, two, one* discovery –
backseat of your mother's car, windows wound down, *now!*
how if we held our hands there for long enough:
flat, keep them flat, palms to the wind,

    they came back softer, colder, new altogether
    as if the M6 for a second
    went north with our fingers; Manchester, Oxenholme,
    ocean and Ireland on its left, America somewhere behind,
    returning with the gift of Orkney air,
    breeze on a pewter loch
    just south of the Skye of Curr, pines
    mirrored in its surface,
    a skin we could slip on easy as a glove.

All of a Sudden

I run my thumb along the jagged edge of the key
I will remove from the bunch any second now.

We've left Hammersmith, six stops to go,
when a text comes through from my father,

an apology for not meeting me
at the Duke for the United game three years ago tonight

and all of a sudden – because things happen
all of a sudden: like my father breathing

then not breathing, like my father deciding
he might want to die, deciding he definitely wants to die

and everything in between – all of a sudden
the empty flat I'm whizzing towards,

its cupboards and kettle and breadbin and cat
and smell draped over a half-open bedroom door

begin to resemble the tiniest of deaths.
Buckle up, kiddo,

there's light at the end of this swinging carriage
if you'll only crane your neck to see.

My father is sitting on the other side of the french doors

just sitting, like a grizzly bear I shoo away in June.
Back hunched, staring at the ground, a red biro
tucked behind his ear. I like to think
he's marvelling at the patio we dug,
the pebble path I skipped school to help lay,
or planning for another pond, another
row of sunflowers by the wall.
                                          Right on cue
the cat arrives and figure-of-eights a plant pot
as my father itches the back of her neck with the biro,
flicks greenflies from his shirt.
I can never wake early from this dream,
never sprint fast enough down the landing, never
unzip the blinds, swing open the window in time to hear
the thud of his footsteps over the shed roof,
branches bouncing back to stillness.
And I'll never know – how could I? –
that in this dream he'd grow old, grow fur, eventually.
The locals think I'm crazy –
they say you shouldn't feed the bears – *dumb Brit.*
They say a grizzly will return for a lifetime to the spot
it once found food, the exact kink of river,
stubby bush, overflowing garbage can;
but I do it anyway, always at night, barefoot, just in case
he comes, my father, sniffs me out,
calls off this silly game, crosses the Atlantic, Canada –
and I'm already gone –

he'll see my shoes tucked behind the glass,
laces still in a bow,
and he'll think no different; he'll wait, he'll sit,
back hunched, staring at the ground,
till August ends and the bears, wide-eyed,
come for him too.

Shopping for Sunglasses in November

There's a girl from years back
I think about whenever I'm in the queue

for the self-checkout, or brushing my teeth,
or hungover and alone in the house on a Sunday.

Like today, like right now, like the decision that
new sunglasses are the only way I'll finish this poem –

so here I am, three floors above Oxford, deep
in the belly of Debenhams, following a line

of buggy-mums through another set of double-doors.
They are like lives, the sunglasses.

And like lives I try them on,
settling for a pair of lime-green Ray-Bans.

For a second I consider it – thumbing to her number on my phone –
sprinting out of here, alarm wailing,

tattooed security too slow for this new life, recently
acquired, emitting light, and with so much more to tell you.

Leaves

Not for the first time this week
I pace the flat we used to share,
marking every imperfection
with a post-it note. I crouch by the fridge,
lie flat, one ear to the tiles,
or drag another chair to reach
a spider's web, an Australia of mould.

I catch a bus one stop in the hope
you'll be there when I get back,
face peering from behind the sofa,
body at home in the forest I made.
I drop the shopping at the door.
Your hand half remembering how to beckon,
your fingers rooting in my hair.

The First and Last Day of Everything
For Danny Carrick

One Saturday morning before anyone was up
I filled a fist with coppers from the jar
by the front door, then on tiptoes,
slid your leather jacket
from its hook, stood for a second
with its weight, slipped
inside naked in front of the mirror
and emptied the coins into the left-hand pocket
stuffed with a Sainsbury's receipt and an orange train ticket.
Clink, clink, clink.

Two decades gone and I'm still asking: what did they really see,
the goldfish, those sparrows on the feeder?
What of the day moon? The television?
What if every singing coin I counted
back into that jar was rain
falling on the stillest lake that was all of our futures?
Yes, maybe they know;
just sunlight spilling in through a back window
and a boy marching about the living room
in his father's leather jacket.

Ross 154

> *Ross 154 is a star in the southern zodiac constellation of Sagittarius. It has an apparent visual magnitude of 10.44, making it much too faint to be seen with the naked eye.* – Wikipedia

The only Ross I ever knew was the bloke in The Duke:
corner of the bar opposite the Guinness tap
so when you walked in you walked right past him.
Best view of the window he said.

We came to know him, my sister and I, by his greetings:
either a wink or a grunt or nothing at all depending on
what my father called *the horses that day*.
When I'm back one weekend and the stool is empty,

a different face behind the bar, the pool table
gutted and legless in the garden, whispers of *a sale*
I realise you, Ross – the pieces of you:
wooden stick, flat cap, hung green jacket grazing the floor

barely hiding the offie bag of John Smith's for later –
were a constellation I had never noticed.
But most of all you were a glance, a shuffle,
a childhood of World Cups, sticky carpet, Mum's cigarette breath

captured in half-a-second of eye contact
each time that black Volvo pulled up, edged its way
across the window you'd faced so stubbornly – *Up we get*.
Two pints in and I've spotted you in the glass,

shoulders hunched over a Guinness. You wink.
Two children shoot past and into the garden.
'Another, please.' The pint, three-quarters-full,
settles to starless while I pay.

Lop Nur

My father dives headfirst into a lake,
swims till his pink shoulders become stars.
He swims for days, beach to beach.

The pink shoulders of my father's stars
are attached to other stars by invisible rope.
Birds perch on them. Cranes and gulls

and bony blue herons appear at 6 a.m.
from behind the mountain, slipping
like moons, more the more you look.

My headfirst dive's no match.
Feel the gulp that's coming, barnacle-
chinned, the birds inexplicably lifting.

Moonless June

For weeks they arrive out of the Arctic Ocean,
watched by a grizzly momma and her cubs,
my father in a sky blue suit,
long sideburns, Elvis Costello glasses,
my giggling sister on his shoulders.
For weeks they cross the beach. For weeks
they reach the treeline, my sister
an old woman and my father a baby
swaddled in the suit. She rests for breath,
leans her one free arm against a boulder. The cubs
have stopped noticing; momma drinks
from a stream, paws at the moonless water.
My sister drops the suit, hears it land, breathes
like a woman I have never met.

When you lean close and tell me

not a day goes by that you don't think of him
but you're thinking less now and you hope this is a sign
I pick at the grass and remember all the people

I've thought about since this conversation started –
an ex from school, Sylvia upstairs, the postman.
When I exit the roundabout behind an ASDA lorry

it's not the A342 Northbound I'm driving on but the
freckled curve of my father's spine. When a stranger
spots them from a layby, points with a gloved hand

to the horses drinking from the lake of my father's face
I climb the field to get a better view. In the valley
two leafless trees fill with light, become lungs.

Feathers

The Panasonic radio I ordered for you is still boxed
in the corner under a mug and a film of dust.
When I unlock the french doors a hinge sticks

and the cat looks too but loses interest.
They are still falling this morning,
feathers a foot thick on the patio.

Why only now, in this smeary glass, does your voice
return, making perfect sense
of light fallen too fast from a sun that, just yesterday

had disappeared, eclipsed, as the Radio 4 presenter said,
'by a cloud of beating wings the size of Reading'?
So, when did you decide? Was it after the pub?

After I finished my Guinness, refused another drink,
took our glasses to the bar and nodded at the man
underneath the flat screen television?

They must have known more than they let on,
the birds. You would probably laugh, both hands
deep in your pockets and looking up as you do.

Because, Dad, I've got this radio I can't give you
and there's a wheelbarrow in my garden
full to bursting with feathers I didn't ask for.

The Secret

You only smoked at midnight,
the back door ajar –
moon in the bevelled glass,
a tap, footsteps, the latch. Some nights
I could hear meteors from my bed,
and still, the television, CNN,
the muffled fucks or a cough;
every boom and crackle
of every crater opening up in the carpet.

Yes, it rained, one morning,
when I asked, 'Dad, what's lithium?'
and you bolted then re-bolted
the kitchen window.
I might have believed lithium was a small bird
or a smell that glass couldn't keep out,
or in.

Impacts

It happens next summer when the car in front turns left
at the motel sign and a doe notices just in time
to blink and a man with a bag of beers looks
but doesn't slow any.
Or tonight, when I wake
to your naked arm cold and too heavy
so my breath holds as I pretend not to feel, pretend
I didn't catch its eye and, for a second
consider braking left
on a year I'm yet to live. It happens
on a bridge over a train track, a father back for a weekend, a son
propped on the railings
arms in a V, altogether unaware of the light's red to amber,
the freight around the bend, its horn
an impact that will whoosh through him, keep him
quiet all the way home
up there on his father's shoulders.

Acknowledgements

Thanks are due to the editors of the following journals and anthologies where some of these poems, or versions of them, first appeared: *Brittle Star*, *Crannóg*, *Everything That Can Happen*: *Poems about the Future* (The Emma Press, 2019), *Ink, Sweat, and Tears*, *The Interpreter's House*, *Magma*, *The Manchester Review*, *The North*, *PN Review*, *The Poetry Shed*. I am grateful to The University of Manchester's Centre for New Writing for a generous bursary in 2017. Special thanks to Vona Groarke and John McAuliffe without whose love and time over the years these poems would not exist; to everyone at The Poetry Business, Suzannah Evans and Eleanor Holmshaw in particular; to my Godmother, Elizabeth Garrett; to my Mum, who sees everything first.